FUN WITH MATH
Adding

A Crabtree Roots Book

DOUGLAS BENDER

Crabtree Publishing
crabtreebooks.com

School-to-Home Support for Caregivers and Teachers

This book helps children grow by letting them practice reading. Here are a few guiding questions to help the reader with building his or her comprehension skills. Possible answers appear here in red.

Before Reading:

• What do I think this book is about?
  - *I think this book is about math and adding.*
  - *I think this book is about how to add.*

• What do I want to learn about this topic?
  - *I want to learn what adding is.*
  - *I want to learn how to add numbers together.*

During Reading:

• I wonder why...
  - *I wonder why people might need calculators to add.*
  - *I wonder why people use a plus sign when they add.*

• What have I learned so far?
  - *I have learned that addition tells us how many there are.*
  - *I have learned that people use a plus sign when they add numbers together.*

After Reading:

• What details did I learn about this topic?
  - *I have learned that people use addition all the time.*
  - *I have learned that adding is a faster way to count things.*

• Read the book again and look for the vocabulary words.
  - *I see the word **crayon** on page 4 and the words **plus sign** on page 8. The other vocabulary words are found on page 14.*

1+1= 2+2=

2+3= 3+4=

Addition helps us find out how many there are.

Find one red **crayon**, and one blue crayon.

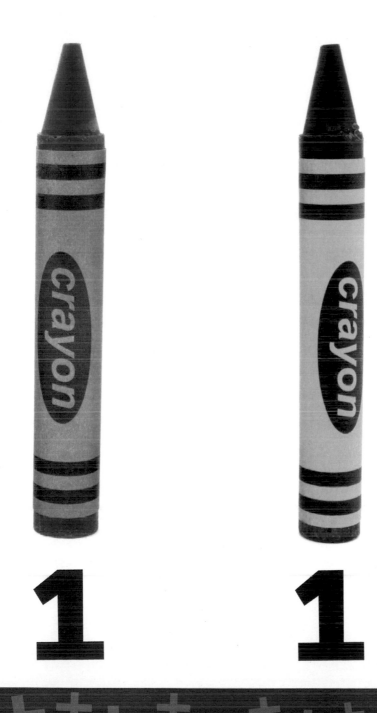

1   1

Now you have two crayons!

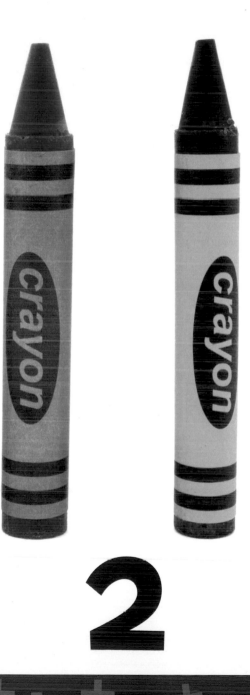

2

You can use a **plus sign** to add two numbers.

1 + 1

One **apple** plus two apples is three apples.

3

We use **math** all
the time!

+ 2

= 4

Word List
Sight Words

a	have	out	two
all	helps	red	us
and	how	the	use
are	many	there	we
blue	now	three	you
find	one	time	

Words to Know

addition

apple

crayon

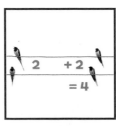

math

plus sign

46 Words

Addition helps us find out how many there are.

Find one red **crayon**, and one blue crayon.

Now you have two crayons!

You can use a **plus sign** to add two numbers.

One **apple** plus two apples is three apples.

We use **math** all the time!

FUN WITH MATH
Adding

Crabtree Publishing

crabtreebooks.com   800-387-7650

Hardcover	978-1-4271-5626-6
Paperback	978-1-4271-5632-7
Ebook (pdf)	978-1-4271-3348-9
Epub	978-1-4271-3408-0
Read-along	978-1-4271-5650-1
Audio book	978-1-0396-0441-4

Printed in Canada/072023/CPC20230728

Library and Archives Canada Cataloguing in Publication
Title: Adding / Douglas Bender.
Names: Bender, Douglas, 1992- author.
Description: Series statement: Fun with math |
   "A Crabtree roots book".
Identifiers: Canadiana (print) 20210195770 |
   Canadiana (ebook) 20210195789 |
   ISBN 9781427156266 (hardcover) |
   ISBN 9781427156327 (softcover) |
   ISBN 9781427133489 (HTML) |
   ISBN 9781427134080 (EPUB) |
   ISBN 9781427156501 (read-along ebook)
Subjects: LCSH: Addition—Juvenile literature.
Classification: LCC QA115 .B46 2022 | DDC j513.2/11—dc23

Published in Canada
Crabtree Publishing
616 Welland Avenue
St. Catharines, Ontario
L2M 5V6

Published in the United States
Crabtree Publishing
347 Fifth Avenue
Suite 1402-145
New York, NY 10016

Written by: Douglas Bender
Designed by: Rhea Wallace
Series Development: James Earley
Proofreader: Janine Deschenes
Educational Consultant: Marie Lemke M.Ed.
Photographs: Shutterstock: Kletr: cover; Freer:
p. 3, 14; Lucie Lang: p. 5, 7, 9, 14; Nataly Studio:
p. 10, 11; Bachkova Natalia; p. 12, 13, 14.

Library of Congress Cataloging-in-Publication Data
Names: Bender, Douglas, 1992- author.
Title: Adding / Douglas Bender.
Description: New York, NY : Crabtree Publishing Company, [2022] |
   Series: Fun with math - a Crabtree roots book |
   Includes index.
Identifiers: LCCN 2021017598 (print) |
   LCCN 2021017599 (ebook) |
   ISBN 9781427156266 (hardcover) |
   ISBN 9781427156327 (paperback) |
   ISBN 9781427133489 (ebook) |
   ISBN 9781427134080 (epub) |
   ISBN 9781427156501
Subjects: LCSH: Addition--Juvenile literature.
Classification: LCC QA115 .B46 2022 (print) |
   LCC QA115 (ebook) | DDC 513.2/11--dc23
LC record available at https://lccn.loc.gov/2021017598
LC ebook record available at https://lccn.loc.gov/2021017599